I0815579

Selena Gomez

Skillful Singer, Actress, & Businesswoman

by Grace Hansen

Abdo Kids Jumbo is an Imprint of Abdo Kids
abdobooks.com

abdobooks.com

Published by Abdo Kids, a division of ABDO, P.O. Box 398166, Minneapolis, Minnesota 55439.

Printed in the United States of America, North Mankato, Minnesota.

052024

092024

Photo Credits: Alamy, Everette Collection, Getty Images, Shutterstock

Production Contributors: Teddy Borth, Jennie Forsberg, Grace Hansen
Design Contributors: Candice Keimig, Pakou Moua

Library of Congress Control Number: 2023948705

Publisher's Cataloging-in-Publication Data

Names: Hansen, Grace, author.

Title: Selena Gomez: skillful singer, actress, & businesswoman / by Grace Hansen

Other title: skillful singer, actress, & businesswoman

Description: Minneapolis, Minnesota : Abdo Kids, 2025 | Series: Leading biographies | Includes online resources and index.

Identifiers: ISBN 9798384900771 (lib. bdg.) | ISBN 9798384901471 (ebook) | ISBN 9798384901822 (Read-to-me eBook)

Subjects: LCSH: Gomez, Selena, 1992---Juvenile literature. | Women singers--United States--Biography--Juvenile literature. | Actresses--Biography--Juvenile literature. | Businesswomen--Biography--Juvenile literature.

Classification: DDC 791.43092--dc23

Table of Contents

Selena's Beginnings

Selena Marie Gomez was born on July 22, 1992, in Grand Prairie, Texas. When Selena was 5, her parents divorced. She spent most of her childhood with her mother and grandparents.

Grand Prairie
THEO'S
DRIVE-IN
ROOT BEER
HAMBURGERS
VEHICULOS
ACEPTAMOS
Texas

Selena was a natural performer from a young age. Her first TV role was on *Barney & Friends*. She danced and sang on the show for 2 years.

Disney Star

When Selena was 12, she **auditioned** for the Disney Channel. She got a few roles on big TV series. In 2006, she appeared in one episode of *The Suite Life of Zack & Cody*. She went on to play Mikayla on *Hannah Montana*.

Hannah Montana TV series

Finally, in 2007, Selena landed a lead role. She played Alex Russo on *Wizards of Waverly Place* until 2012. The series finale was the most-watched final episode of any Disney Channel show.

Music and the Big Screen

In 2008, Selena decided to start a pop rock band. Selena Gomez & the Scene's first album was called *Kiss & Tell*. The band released two more albums in 2010 and 2011.

TEEN
CHOICE
2011

Selena appeared on the big screen for the first time in *Ramona & Beezus*. Selena went on to appear in both **comedies** and **dramas**. This helped grow her acting skills.

In July 2013, Selena released her solo **debut** album, *Stars Dance*. Her second album, *Revival*, came out in 2015. Fans couldn't get enough of the **singles** "Same Old Love" and "Come and Get It."

Rare, Selena's third studio album, dropped in January 2020. "Lose You to Love Me" was Selena's first number-one **single** in the US. In September, Selena launched her makeup company Rare Beauty.

USE KIND WORDS.
IT'S AS EASY AS
APPLYING LIPSTICK.
Gifted
Fun

The Triple Threat

Many journalists have called Gomez a “triple threat.” But she has proven to be even more than a singer, performer, and actor. Fans are excited to see if there’s anything Selena can’t do!

Career Highlights

2007 Selena stars as Alex Russo in *Wizards of Waverly Place* from 2007 to 2012.

May 2015 Selena plays a villain in Taylor Swift's music video "Bad Blood."

October 2015 Selena signs on as **executive producer** of the television series *13 Reasons Why*.

August 2020 Selena executive produces and hosts the television cooking show *Selena + Chef*.

September 2020 Selena makes *Time* magazine's list of the 100 most influential people.

2021 Gomez executive produces and stars in the television series *Only Murders in the Building*.

2022 Selena releases her documentary film *Selena Gomez: My Mind & Me*.

2023 Selena is nominated for a Golden Globe for her role in *Only Murders in the Building*.

Glossary

auditioned – tried out for a role or position by performing.

comedy – a play, film, story, or television show that is funny or happy.

debut – relating to a first appearance.

drama – a television show or film that is serious in nature and reveals emotional conflicts among fictional characters.

executive producer – the person who heads the production of a film or television show and whose main job is to find and secure money and talent for the project.

single – a track released separately from an album.

Index

Visit **abdokids.com** to access crafts, games, videos, and more!

Use Abdo Kids code

LSK0771

or scan this QR code!